Macmillan/McGraw-Hill TIMELINKS

People and Places

PROGRAM AUTHORS
James A. Banks
Kevin P. Colleary
Linda Greenow
Walter C. Parker
Emily M. Schell
Dinah Zike

CONTRIBUTORS
Raymond C. Jones
Irma M. Olmedo

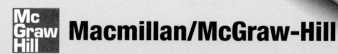
Macmillan/McGraw-Hill

History

PROGRAM AUTHORS

James A. Banks, Ph.D.
Kerry and Linda Killinger Professor
  of Diversity Studies and Director, Center
  for Multicultural Education
University of Washington
Seattle, Washington

Kevin P. Colleary, Ed.D.
Curriculum and Teaching Department
Graduate School of Education
Fordham University
New York, New York

Linda Greenow, Ph.D.
Associate Professor and Chair
Department of Geography
State University of New York at New Paltz
New Paltz, New York

Walter C. Parker, Ph.D.
Professor of Social Studies Education,
  Adjunct Professor of Political Science
University of Washington
Seattle, Washington

Emily M. Schell, Ed.D.
Visiting Professor, Teacher Education
San Diego State University
San Diego, California

Dinah Zike
Educational Consultant
Dinah-Mite Activities, Inc.
San Antonio, Texas

CONTRIBUTORS

Raymond C. Jones, Ph.D.
Director of Secondary Social Studies
  Education
Wake Forest University
Winston-Salem, North Carolina

Irma M. Olmedo
Associate Professor
University of Illinois-Chicago
College of Education
Chicago, Illinois

HISTORIANS/SCHOLARS

Ned Blackhawk
Associate Professor of History
  and American Indian Studies
University of Wisconsin
Madison, Wisconsin

Jeffrey D. Long, Ph.D.
Associate Professor of Religious
  and Asian Studies
Elizabethtown College
Elizabethtown, Pennsylvania

Oscar J. Martinez, Ph.D.
Regents Professor of History
University of Arizona
Tucson, Arizona

GRADE LEVEL REVIEWERS

Kathleen Clark
Second Grade Teacher
Edison Elementary
Fraser, Michigan

Patricia Hinchliff
Second Grade Teacher
West Woods School
Hamden, Connecticut

Pamela South
Second Grade Teacher
Greenwood Elementary School
Princess Anne, Maryland

Karen Starr
Second Grade Teacher
Arthur Froberg Elementary School
Rockford, Illinois

EDITORIAL ADVISORY BOARD

Bradley R. Bakle
Assistant Superintendent
East Allen County Schools
New Haven, Indiana

Marilyn Barr
Assistant Superintendent for Instruction
Clyde-Savannah Central School
Clyde, New York

Lisa Bogle
Elementary Coordinator, K-5
Rutherford County Schools
Murfreesboro, Tennessee

Janice Buselt
Campus Support, Primary and ESOL
Wichita Public Schools
Wichita, Kansas

Kathy Cassioppi
Social Studies Coordinator
Rockford Public Schools, District 205
Rockford, Illinois

Denise Johnson, Ph.D.
Social Studies Supervisor
Knox County Schools
Knoxville, Tennessee

Steven Klein, Ph.D.
Social Studies Coordinator
Illinois School District U-46
Elgin, Illinois

Sondra Markman
Curriculum Director
Warren Township Board of Education
Warren Township, New Jersey

Cathy Nelson
Social Studies Coordinator
Columbus Public Schools
Columbus, Ohio

Holly Pies
Social Studies Coordinator
Vigo County Schools
Terre Haute, Indiana

Avon Ruffin
Social Studies County Supervisor
Winston-Salem/Forsyth Schools
Lewisville, North Carolina

Chuck Schierloh
Social Studies Curriculum Team Leader
Lima City Schools
Lima, Ohio

Bob Shamy
Social Studies Supervisor
East Brunswick Public Schools
East Brunswick, New Jersey

Judy Trujillo
Social Studies Coordinator
Columbia Missouri School District
Columbia, Missouri

Gayle Voyles
Director of the Center for Economic
  Education
Kansas City School District
Kansas City, Missouri

Todd Wigginton
Coordinator of Social Studies K-12
Metropolitan Nashville Public Schools
Nashville, Tennessee

The McGraw·Hill Companies

Macmillan McGraw-Hill

Copyright © 2009 by The McGraw-Hill Companies, Inc. All rights reserved. Except as permitted under the United States Copyright Act, no part of this publication may be reproduced or distributed in any form or by any means, or stored in a database or retrieval system, without prior permission of the publisher.
Send all inquires to: Macmillan/McGraw-Hill, 8787 Orion Place, Columbus, OH 43240-4027

MHID 0-02-152401-7   ISBN 978-0-02-152401-3   Printed in the United States of America

6 7 8 9 10 QVR / LEH 13 12 11

People and Places

Table of Contents

Unit 3 Long Ago and Today

 How did people from long ago make a difference?

Skills and Features

Maps

EXPLORE The Big Idea

How did people
from long ago
make a difference?

LOG ON Find out more about people
long ago at
www.macmillanmh.com

Long Ago and Today

People, Places, and Events

Paul Revere

Paul Revere was an American hero.

Paul Revere's House

Paul Revere's **house** is in Boston, Massachusetts.

Paul Revere's Midnight Ride

Paul Revere warned others that British soldiers were coming. This was called **Paul Revere's Midnight Ride**.

Vocabulary

past

transportation

communication

Reading Skill

Compare and Contrast

Different Alike Different

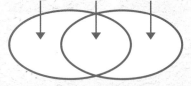

Communities
Then and Now

Home Life

Long ago, most families lived on farms. They cooked over fires. They grew food in gardens. They carried water in buckets from wells.

Today, we cook with a stove or oven. We shop for food at a store. Water and electricity run right into our homes.

 How did people get food and water long ago?

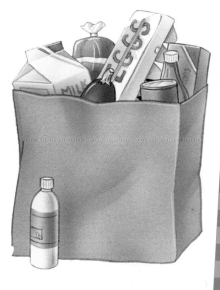

Getting Around

In the **past**, most families stayed near their homes. Past means long ago. Families mostly visited places they could walk to, like neighbors' homes. Sometimes it was a long walk to school or church.

Horses pulled families in carts or wagons for short trips. If a family had to travel to a faraway place, they often went by boat.

Transportation is faster and easier today than it was in the past. Transportation is the way people move from one place to another. Cars, trains, and buses carry families from place to place. Some families take long trips on airplanes.

 What might transportation be like years from now?

Staying in Touch

In the past, **communication** took a long time. Communication is the way people share ideas, thoughts, or information.

People wrote letters to stay in touch. But, it took days to ride a horse across the country to deliver the mail. It took weeks for ships to carry letters across the sea.

Today, letters travel fast on airplanes. E-mail on computers goes around the world in less than a minute.

 How do you communicate?

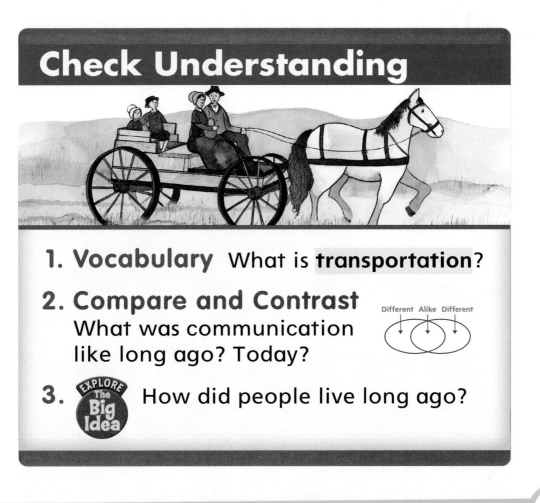

Check Understanding

1. **Vocabulary** What is **transportation**?

2. **Compare and Contrast** What was communication like long ago? Today?

   Different Alike Different

3. **EXPLORE The Big Idea** How did people live long ago?

Early Americans

Lesson 2

Vocabulary

Native American

settler

Pilgrim

colony

Reading Skill

Compare and Contrast

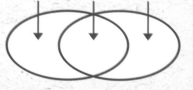

Different Alike Different

Wampanoag mother and daughter

10

Native Americans

Native Americans were the first people to live in America. They are also called American Indians. There are many different groups of American Indians. Each group has its own kind of home, food, and clothing. Each group has its own language and traditions, too.

What are the names of some Native American groups?

Makah

Hopi

Cheyenne

Chippewa

Wampanoag

Cherokee

Timucuan

Settlers from Spain

For a long time, Native Americans were the only people living here. Then **settlers** arrived from Spain. A settler is a person who moves from one place to live in another place.

A Native American group called the Timucuan lived in Florida. That is where the first Spanish settlers arrived. The Timucuan grew many vegetables.

The Timucuan planted corn, pumpkins, and squash.

Today, St. Augustine, Florida, is the oldest city in the United States.

The Spanish settlers wanted the land for themselves. They forced the Timucuan to leave. They built a town called St. Augustine.

 What country did the first settlers come from?

Places
The Oldest Schoolhouse

This school was built in St. Augustine about 300 years ago. It is the oldest school in the United States.

Pilgrims from England

The **Pilgrims** were a group of people from England who traveled to America. They started a **colony** named Plymouth. A colony is a place that is ruled by another country. Plymouth was ruled by the King of England.

A Native American named Squanto knew how to speak English. He showed the Pilgrims how to fish, hunt, and grow food. By fall they had plenty to eat.

The Pilgrims had a special meal to thank God for all the good things that had happened. Every year we celebrate this event on Thanksgiving Day.

 How did Squanto help the Pilgrims?

Check Understanding

1. **Vocabulary** Who are the **Native Americans**?

2. **Compare and Contrast** How were the Spanish settlers and English Pilgrims alike? Different?

   Different Alike Different

3. What do we celebrate on Thanksgiving Day?

Use Map Scales

Vocabulary

map scale

This map of Florida has a **map scale**. A map scale tells the distance between places on a map. Find the map scale on the next page.

1. Place a strip of paper between St. Augustine and Gainesville. First draw a mark where St. Augustine is on the strip of paper. Then mark where Gainesville is.

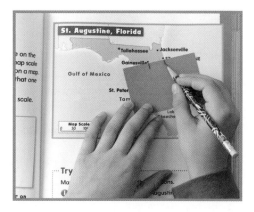

2. Place the strip of paper on the map scale. Put one of the marks at zero. You will see that St. Augustine is about 50 miles from Gainesville.

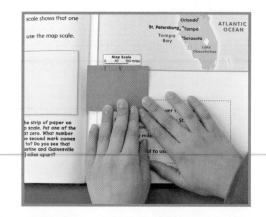

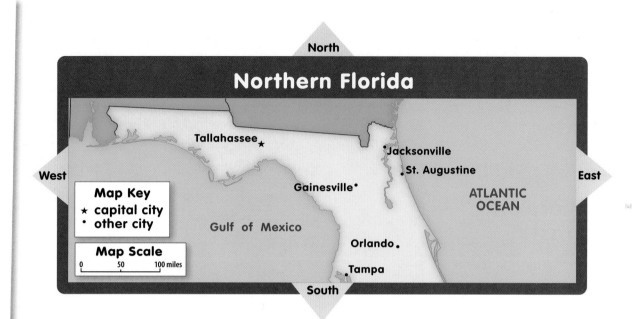

North

Northern Florida

West

Tallahassee ★

•Jacksonville

•St. Augustine

Gainesville•

ATLANTIC OCEAN

East

Map Key
★ capital city
• other city

Gulf of Mexico

Orlando •

Map Scale
0   50   100 miles

•Tampa

South

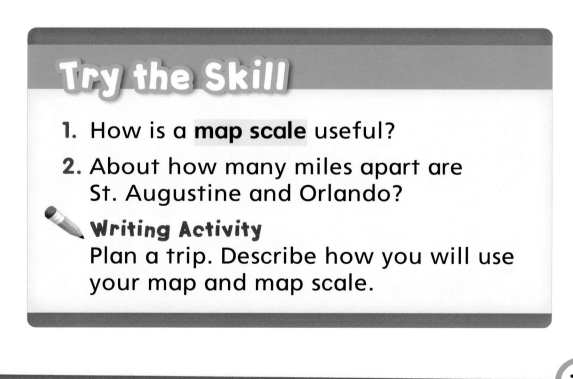

Try the Skill

1. How is a **map scale** useful?

2. About how many miles apart are St. Augustine and Orlando?

Writing Activity
Plan a trip. Describe how you will use your map and map scale.

Colonies to States

Vocabulary

President

Reading Skill

Compare and Contrast

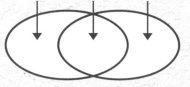

Different Alike Different

King George III of England

18

13 Colonies

More settlers came to America from England. Soon there were 13 colonies. King George III of England was the leader of the colonies.

People grew tired of following King George's rules. They wanted to be free to choose their own way of life.

Who was the leader of the 13 colonies?

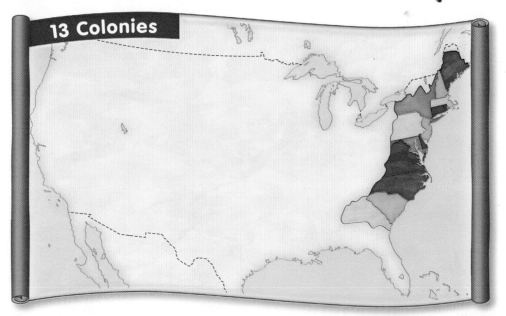
13 Colonies

Standing Up for Freedom

A man named Paul Revere lived in the colony of Massachusetts. He found out that England was sending soldiers with guns to the colonies.

Paul Revere cared about the people in the colonies. He rode his horse from town to town, warning them.

A year later, on July 4, 1776, leaders from the 13 colonies got together. They signed a paper called the Declaration of Independence. It said they would not follow the rules of the King of England.

 What did the Declaration of Independence say?

Around the World

People in Egypt celebrate Revolution Day on July 23. They wanted freedom from England, just like people in the 13 colonies did.

1775

Paul Revere rides to warn Americans that British soldiers are coming.

1776

American leaders sign the Declaration of Independence.

Fighting for Freedom

The 13 colonies had a war with England. George Washington was America's leader. Just like Revere, Washington was a hero.

After many years, America won the war. Each colony became a state. The new states became the United States of America.

After the war, the people wanted George Washington to become the leader of the new country. George Washington became the first **President** of the United States.

What happened in 1776?

America wins the war against England.

George Washington becomes first President of the United States.

Check Understanding

1. **Vocabulary** What is a **President**?

2. **Compare and Contrast**
   How were Paul Revere and George Washington alike? Different?

   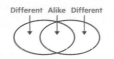

3. How did the leaders of the colonies make a difference?

Lesson 4

Vocabulary
pioneer

Reading Skill
Compare and Contrast

Different   Alike   Different

Families on the Move

24

Moving West

People in the 13 new states wanted more land. Settlers began to move west. They were called **pioneers**. Pioneers are people who leave home to lead the way into a new land.

Driving covered wagons over rivers and mountains was hard for the pioneers. Often they got sick or lost. Sometimes Native Americans attacked them.

 Why did the pioneers move?

People
Daniel Boone

Daniel Boone was a pioneer in Kentucky. He said, "I was happy in the midst of dangers. . . ."

Dangerous Trails

Native Americans were forced to move to make room for the pioneers. President Andrew Jackson made them give up their land and leave their homes.

One group that moved was the Cherokee. Many Cherokee families walked from Georgia all the way to Oklahoma.

The Cherokee called this walk "the place where they cried." Today it is called the *Trail of Tears*.

 Why were Native Americans forced to move?

Check Understanding

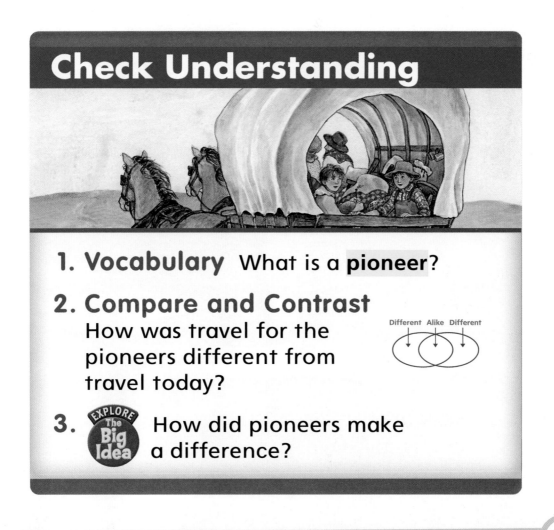

1. **Vocabulary** What is a **pioneer**?

2. **Compare and Contrast** How was travel for the pioneers different from travel today?

    Different Alike Different

3. **EXPLORE The Big Idea** How did pioneers make a difference?

Vocabulary

interview

slavery

Reading Skill

Compare and Contrast

Different   Alike   Different

Freedom for All

A Family Long Ago

To **interview** means to ask a person questions and write down the answers. Wanda interviewed her grandma about their family's past.

Wanda How did our family live long ago?

Grandma Long ago we were not free. Our family lived in **slavery**. Slavery means that another person takes away your freedom and forces you to work for no pay.

 What is slavery?

Becoming Free

Wanda How did our family become free?

Grandma Well, to tell you the truth, they just took their freedom back! A brave woman named Harriet Tubman helped them escape on the Underground Railroad. The Underground Railroad was not a train, it was a trail.

Wanda What did our family do when they became free?

Grandma They worked to help more and more people be free.

Wanda When did all the people become free?

Grandma It took a long time! First, President Abraham Lincoln said that slavery was against the law. He said that all people are free.

 What did President Lincoln say about slavery?

Event
Escape to Freedom

Many men and women escaped from slavery on the Underground Railroad. They followed guides by night and hid by day.

The American Civil War

A Fight to End Slavery

Wanda Did that end slavery forever?

Grandma It should have! But it didn't. Sorry to tell you, but it took a war. When people who live in the same country fight against each other, it is called a civil war. Some states in the North were against slavery. Some states in the South wanted to keep slavery.

Wanda Who won the war?

Grandma The North won the war in 1865. After the war ended, slavery in the United States ended. At long last, African Americans were free.

 How did slavery end forever?

Check Understanding

1. **Vocabulary** How did Wanda **interview** her grandma?

2. **Compare and Contrast** How were Tubman and Lincoln alike? Different?

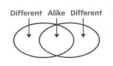

3. How did Harriet Tubman help Wanda's family long ago?

Citizenship

Points of View

Why should people be free?

These second graders are from Raleigh, North Carolina. Read about why they think people should be free.

Raleigh, North Carolina

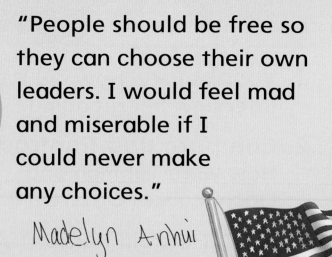

"People should be free so they can choose their own leaders. I would feel mad and miserable if I could never make any choices."

Madelyn Anhui

Madelyn Anhui

"It isn't good when people are always being told what to do, and they can never say what they think. It is important for everyone to be respected and their feelings to be respected."

Aris Najafi

Aris Najafi

"People should be free because all people are the same except on the outside. If I couldn't make choices, I would feel sad and lonely and left out."

Casey Riemann

Casey Riemann

Unit 3 Review and Assess

Vocabulary

Number a paper from I to 3. Next to each number write the word that matches the meaning.

communication   **settler**   **colony**

1. a person who moves from one place to live in another place

2. a place that is ruled by another country

3. the way people share ideas, thoughts, or information

Critical Thinking

4. How did the 13 colonies become the United States of America?

5. How did the Trail of Tears change life for some Cherokee families?

Use Map Scales

Look at the map of Connecticut below. Use the map scale, a strip of paper, and a pencil to answer the question.

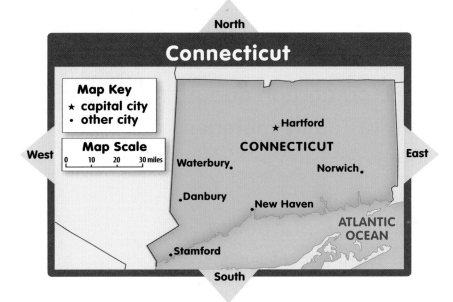

6. How far is it from New Haven to Danbury?

A. about 5 miles

B. about 10 miles

C. about 20 miles

D. about 30 miles

The Big Idea History Activity

Make a Puppet

1. Interview an older relative to learn about a family member from long ago.

2. Write a paragraph about how that family member made a difference.

3. Make a stick puppet of that family member. Use doll clothes, yarn, glue, or other things you can find.

4. Use your puppet to read your paragraph to your class.

Picture Glossary

C

colony A place that is ruled by another country. *The city of St. Augustine, Florida, was once a Spanish colony.* (page 14)

communication The way people share ideas, thoughts, or information. *E-mail is a kind of communication.* (page 8)

I

interview To ask a person questions and write down the answers. *I will interview my grandma about our family's past.* (page 29)

M

map scale The part of a map that tells the distance between places. *This map scale shows that one inch equals 100 miles.* (page 16)

N

Native American One of the first people to live in America, also called an American Indian. *Each Native American group had its own kind of homes, tools, and clothing.* (page 11)

past Long ago. *In the **past,** families used to get from place to place in a wagon pulled by horses.* (page 6)

Pilgrim A person from England who traveled to America. *The **Pilgrims** left their country to find a better life in America.* (page 14)

pioneer A person who leaves home to lead the way into a new land. *Many **pioneers** moved west in covered wagons to find new homes.* (page 25)

President The leader of our country. *George Washington was the first **President** of our country.* (page 22)

settler A person who moves from one place to live in another place. *This Spanish **settler** lived in the state of California.* (page 12)

slavery When one person forces another to work without pay. *Our family once lived in slavery, but today they are free.* (page 29)

T

transportation The way people move from one place to another. *Transportation today is faster than it was long ago.* (page 7)

Index

This index lists many things you can find in your book. It tells the page numbers on which they are found. If you see the letter *m* before a page number, you will find a map on that page.

Credits